DETROIT PUBLIC LIBRARY
3 5674 02586300 3
W9-BXS-576

KISHINA

by
Maxine Rock

Epilogues by Dr. Terry Maple and Gerald Lentz

PEACHTREE PUBLISHERS
ATLANTA

This book is dedicated
to my favorite young primates,

Lauren Rock and **Michael Rock**.

Thank you for being such wonderful offspring.

Published by
Peachtree Publishers, Ltd.
494 Armour Circle NE
Atlanta, Georgia 30324

Jacket and book design by Regina Dalton-Fischel

Manufactured in the United States of America

10 9 8 7 6 5 4 3 2 1

First edition

Library of Congress Cataloguing-in-Publication Data
Rock, Maxine A., 1940-
Kishina : a true story of gorilla survival / Maxine Rock ; epilogues by Terry Maple and Gerald Lentz.
p.cm.
Summary: An account of the first baby gorilla born at the Yerkes Regional Primate Research Center, her various social encounters, and her move to Busch Gardens' Myombe Reserve.
ISBN 1-56145-107-X (pbk.)
1. Gorilla—Georgia—Atlanta—Biography—Juvenile literature. 2. Gorilla—Florida—Tampa—Biography—Juvenile literature. 3. Yerkes Regional Primate Research Center. 4. Busch Gardens (Tampa. Fla.) [1. Gorilla. 2. Yerkes Regional Primate Research Center. 3. Busch Gardens (Tampa, Fla.)] I. Title.
QL737.P96R63 1995
599.88'46—dc20 95-45789
CIP
AC

Introduction

"Look into the eyes of a gorilla, and you will recognize the distant drumbeat of your own heart."

DR. TERRY MAPLE
DIRECTOR, ZOO ATLANTA

In the hushed jungles of Africa, a huge, dark animal moved slowly in the thick vegetation. As silent as a shadow, the animal pushed aside branches and leaves, making its own path through the rain forest. Nothing stood in the way of this creature. Its arms were as thick as tree trunks, and its body was incredibly powerful. And the face! Seen fleetingly through the trees, partially hidden in the dappled forest light, it was a fierce and frightening sight.

Just a little more than a century ago, most people didn't even know gorillas existed.

This was the gorilla. The first humans who caught a glimpse of it, early in the 1800s, thought they were seeing a monster. Soon stories began to filter out of Africa about hairy, man-like creatures lurking amid the trees. Most people who heard the stories just laughed and said they were tales made to frighten bad children.

Then a medical missionary traveling in Africa also saw one of these mysterious creatures and shot it. Now there was a body to prove the stories were true. Hunters from around the world rushed to Africa for a chance to shoot a "monster ape." One of these hunters described gorillas as "hideous" and said seeing one was "as awful as a nightmare."

Scientists were interested in studying this "nightmare," so they also invaded the gorilla's forest home.

One of the scientists, R. L. Garner, tried to study live gorillas by living in an iron cage in the forest for several months, hoping the animals would pass close by. But the shy animals kept their distance, and rumors continued about how horrible and dangerous the hairy monsters were.

By the early 1900s, so many stories about gorillas had circulated in Europe and the United States that there was great public interest in seeing these animals. Groups of men called "collectors" went into the forests with nets and guns, looking for baby gorillas to bring back to zoos and pet shops. When they found a gorilla family, the collectors would shoot the mother and catch the baby as it tumbled from her arms. Since gorillas try to protect one another, other family members would rush to help; the collectors shot them, too.

Because people didn't know how to care for gorillas, very few of these animals survived in captivity.

Most of the baby gorillas captured in this way died of fright or from the shock of being violently separated from their families. Others became sick on the long trip back to cities. The few who made it often moped around in small zoo cages or in people's homes, obviously ill and depressed. People did not know how to take care of gorillas, what to feed them, or what to do with them if they survived and got bigger. Nobody realized how sensitive and easily upset these gentle animals really were. Because of all these problems, very few gorillas were able to live in captivity.

It was not until 1930, when a scientist named Dr. Robert M. Yerkes began a truly scientific study of apes, that we had any solid information about what gorillas were really like. Dr. Yerkes started research that eventually provided much of the information that had always been lacking about gorillas. Even then, and up until recently, nobody understood why these big, strong animals were so delicate and had such a hard time adjusting to captivity. They often could not even mate or take care of their babies.

Kishina was the first baby gorilla born at the Yerkes Regional Primate Research Center of Emory University.

Was there something wrong with their food? Did gorillas hate cages so much that just being in one kept them from having a good life? Perhaps being around people made gorillas forget what they were and turn away from other animals. Could it be noise, or air pollution, or maybe not seeing grass and lots of trees?

It was a mystery that had to be solved. Gorillas were not doing well in captivity, and wild populations in Africa were being wiped out by hunters and habitat destruction. Many people who really cared about gorillas were afraid the species would disappear.

Then Kishina was born, and everything changed.

Kishina was the first baby gorilla born at the Yerkes Regional Primate Research Center. Named after Dr. Yerkes, the center is nestled on the campus of Emory University in Atlanta, Georgia. It is a big, mysterious place, hidden from the main road by a thick forest. You can only get there by going down a narrow, twisting trail that dips and curves through the woods.

At the center, scientists study monkeys and apes. They want to understand the behavior of these animals, and they also are looking for clues to combat disease in humans. The scientists also seek ways to help the animals. In particular, they want to learn how gorillas develop, how they communicate with one another, and why they have reacted so badly to captivity.

Kishina's birth was very important. From the moment she came into the world, she gave scientists answers they needed to help her species. Kishina's life experiences have taught people how to maintain a more natural physical and family environment for captive gorillas. Now, when you see a gorilla in captivity, you'll know that Kishina helped save its life.

Kishina as a mature adult

CHAPTER 1

Kishina's story begins with her parents, Paki and Ozzie.

Paki was born in the wild, but hunters snatched her from her mother's arms when Paki was only one year old. She spent the rest of her youth in captivity, without a normal gorilla family.

Ozoumo, whom everyone called Ozzie, was Paki's mate. He looked fierce and menacing, but he was really very gentle. Ozzie never hurt anyone, human or gorilla, but just to be on the safe side, the scientists did not allow him to stay with Paki, his favorite female. Ozzie was allowed into Paki's cage just long enough to mate. Sometimes, when Ozzie had to leave her, Paki seemed very sad.

Ozzie, Kishina's father

When Paki became pregnant, the Yerkes scientists were filled with both anxiety and hope. They watched her every move nervously. At that time, scientists and veterinarians thought the best way to care for a gorilla mother and her newborn infant was to keep them away from other gorillas. They were especially worried that gorilla fathers might hurt their infants. They thought that since big gorillas sometimes get very excited, a terrible accident might happen to the tiny baby gorilla. So when the time came for Paki's baby to be born, Paki went to a special "maternity cage."

Species Scarcity

Only about 35,000 lowland gorillas and 450 mountain gorillas still roam the world's rain forests. There are only about 500 gorillas in zoos and animal preserves in the whole world. As scientists and veterinarians better understand gorillas, better artificial habitats can be built, where they will be comfortable and happy and more likely to have happy and healthy babies. Having babies—called reproduction—is important because gorillas are an endangered species, and new babies can help prevent gorillas from becoming extinct.

Paki was alone and restless in the maternity cage. She squatted, then stood, then crouched down and waddled from one side of the cage to the other. She grunted softly as the labor pains began. At one point she laid down and strained hard, but nothing happened. She let out a long, whistling sigh, then got up and kept pacing.

Around midnight the scientists noticed a change in Paki's movements. They could tell that the birth fluid was beginning to flow from Paki. They were very excited because this meant the baby was about to be born. About fifteen minutes later the round, wet head of the baby appeared. Breathing heavily, Paki knelt down. Suddenly, the baby emerged and lay gasping on the floor.

The scientists smiled with relief. They decided to name the infant Kishina, which means "the source" in the African language of Swahili. They hoped that by studying this frail, four-pound newborn and watching her grow, they would learn more about gorillas. If they understood gorillas better, perhaps they could help these animals live comfortably in captivity. Contented gorillas would have healthy babies and help save the species from extinction.

The scientists hoped that Kishina would be "the source" of gorilla knowledge for human beings. In

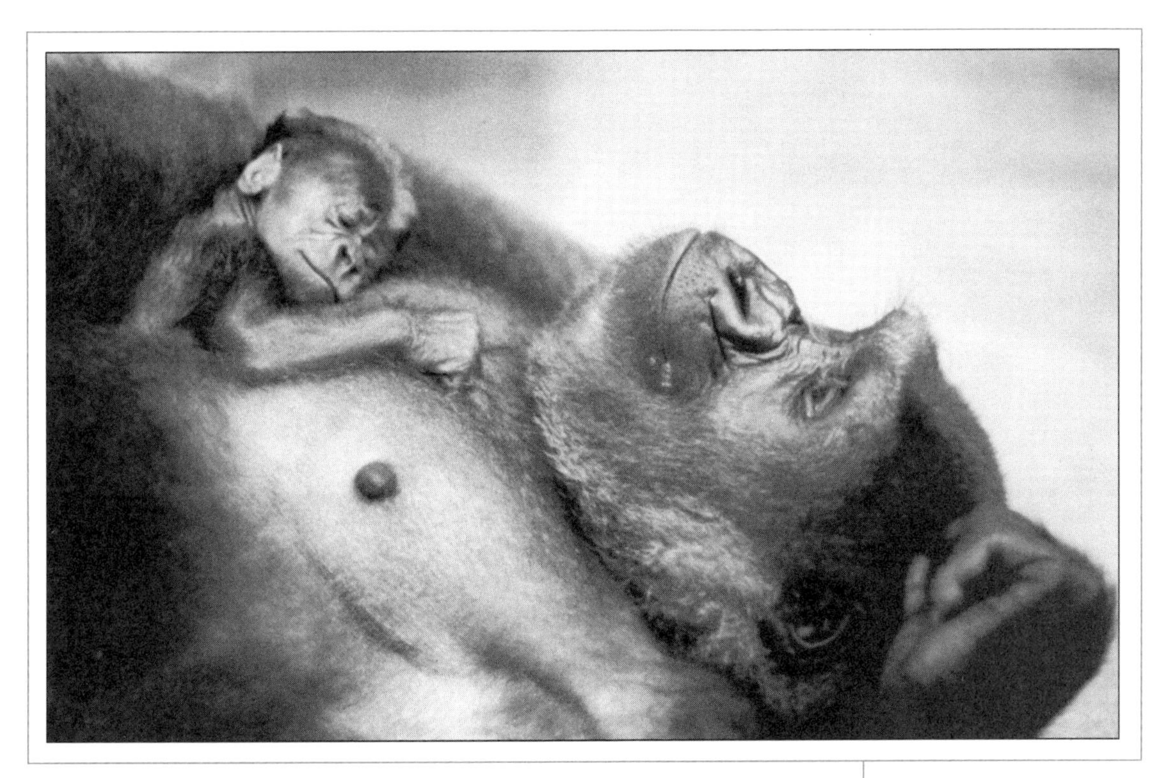

Kishina and Paki rest just after Kishina's birth.

fact, this tiny infant would forever change the way humans and gorillas interacted.

For now, however, Kishina was simply an exhausted infant. She whined, and Paki answered immediately with a deep growl. Then Paki grasped the newborn to her chest and wrapped her arms around the baby. Both of them fell fast asleep on the floor of the cage.

TROUBLE FOR THE NEW BABY

Wild gorilla mothers take very good care of their babies, just like most human mothers. Paki's firm embrace around her baby suggested that she would do the same. Usually gorillas lean on the knuckles of both hands for support when they walk, but when

Paki walked around her cage with Kishina, she used only one hand. With her other hand she kept Kishina pressed tightly against her chest. When Kishina slept, Paki sat in a corner of her cage looking down at her baby with a soft, affectionate gaze. Kishina's tiny red tongue flicked in and out against her mother's cheek in what seemed like a babyish attempt at a kiss.

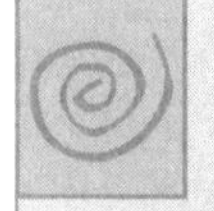

Gorilla Babies

Gorilla babies look almost human. Their heads seem large for their fragile, thin little bodies. Their brown eyes look huge, as if they are trying to stare out at the whole world.

Trouble was not far away, however. After about a week, Paki grew restless. She often seemed irritated by her clinging infant and would put Kishina down on the floor. When that happened, Kishina howled. Paki then paced the floor, sometimes dragging her baby along by one arm as Kishina screamed in fear.

The scientists at Yerkes were worried. They did not know why Paki had suddenly stopped being a good mother. If Paki did not let Kishina nurse, the baby could starve; if she let little Kishina shiver alone on the floor of the cage, Kishina could get very sick. Just like human babies, Kishina needed her mother to take care of her.

A CONFUSED MOTHER

One of the scientists at Yerkes was a man named Ronald Nadler. Dr. Nadler was an expert in animal behavior, with a special interest in gorillas.

Dr. Nadler thought he might know why Paki was acting so strangely. Because Paki had grown up in captivity without a normal gorilla family, she never learned how gorilla parents treat their babies. She had no parenting skills. The scientists separated her from her mate, Ozzie, as well as from the other gorillas to keep her safe, but Dr. Nadler thought Paki's isolation might be making the situation worse. Not only was Paki confused by her baby and her role as a mother, but she was also lonely.

NOBODY SHOULD BE ALONE

Dr. Nadler thought Paki would feel better if she had some company. He asked two of Paki's favorite human caretakers to stay close to her cage. For a little while, this plan worked. Paki began picking up Kishina again and giving her more motherly affection. However, after a few days the caretakers told Dr. Nadler that Paki was once again rejecting her little girl. Dr. Nadler then put some toys in the cage, to distract Paki and give her something to do. She was also moved so her cage was close to other female gorillas. This companionship seemed to make Paki much happier, and for about four days she was good to Kishina.

Despite extra attention and toys, the old restlessness soon returned to Paki. Again, she seemed to be confused about motherhood. Perhaps she was lonely for her mate, Ozzie. Maybe she needed more time to learn how to take care of her baby. But the veterinarians at Yerkes were afraid to wait much longer; they were worried that Kishina might get hurt or become sick with such an inexperienced mother. One day, they slipped into the gorilla cage, wrapped the whimpering infant in a soft blanket, and carried her gently to the Yerkes ape nursery, where she was

NEWBORN GORILLAS

A newborn gorilla has very little hair except for a tuft on the top of the head. As the gorilla grows, hair comes in quickly to cover most of the gorilla's body.

diapered and placed in a plastic crib. Here human hands stroked her tiny head while human arms cuddled her and offered her infant formula from a glass bottle.

A SAD ORPHAN

Gorillas almost always produce single births, but sometimes, twins are born. On August 8, 1994, twin gorillas were born to Pattycake and Tiny Tim at the Bronx Zoo.

Kishina would be safe and warm with her human friends, but she seemed like a sad little orphan. It looked as if she would never be able to grow up as a normal gorilla. Babies (human and gorilla) learn how to behave from their parents or from anybody who takes care of them as a parent would. If Kishina stayed with the humans in the nursery, she might think she should behave like the people who were raising her.

Of course, Kishina could never be a human being, even if she tried to imitate humans. Without the experience of living with a gorilla family, she would not be able to act like an ape, either. She would be an alien in a world of humans, a lonely creature who never belonged anywhere. Saddest of all, when Kishina was old enough to mate and have a baby of her own, she might have the same problems Paki had.

Unfortunately, Kishina's problems were not very unusual. When Kishina was born in the early 1970s, there had been only twenty-nine gorillas born in captivity. Only one of the gorilla mothers had been able to take good care of her baby. The other twenty-eight infants were neglected or abused by their mothers, and one or two had even been killed by the restless, agitated females. If Kishina could be helped to grow up as a normal gorilla who could produce and care for her own offspring, perhaps her experience would help make up for other baby gorillas born in captivity who had not survived. But how could she be normal when she was spending her babyhood in a crib made for humans, instead of in her mother's arms?

Dr. Nadler was upset about having to take Kishina away from her mother. He decided to find a way to teach Kishina how to live with other gorillas and to keep trying to find out why Paki was not a good mother to Kishina.

The Gorilla Group

Gorillas are social animals. In the African forests, their native home, gorillas are never far away from their troop, or family group. Ten or more animals usually make up a gorilla family. It is headed by the oldest and strongest male, called the dominant silverback. He is called a silverback because, as he ages, the hair on his back turns silver, just as human hair turns gray. In addition to the silverback, the family is made up of several females and their offspring and sometimes one or two young males who have not formed their own families yet.

In the wild, the silverback guides his family and watches over them. The mothers and their offspring may eat together, and they sleep close to one another. The troop travels together and takes care to remain within hearing distance. Females watch over one another's youngsters. After a female gives birth, all the others wait for her if she cannot move as quickly. The dominant male decides when the group is ready to move on.

Female gorillas are never alone in the wild because they stay close to the family group, especially to the male they have chosen as mate. If a mate dies, the female will quickly try to find another one. She may leave her family group to do this. Sometimes a female will wander off with a male from another group if she has not had a baby for a long time.

Males may remain with their original family group and take over the leadership role if their father is too old to continue.

However, most of the young males will leave and form troops of their own. Sometimes the dominant male gets jealous of younger males in the group and chases them away. The silverback also scares off strange males who look as if they might lure away the family's females. Most of the time, the adult females in a gorilla group stick together and accept the strongest and smartest as the dominant female or "big mama." This female is usually the first to mate with the silverback, or "big daddy."

Female gorillas are pregnant for about nine months, just like female humans. Usually, a gorilla birth is quicker and seems to be less painful than human birth, and the mother recovers rapidly. Soon after her baby is born, she scoops it into her arms and goes to sit very close to her mate. She makes every effort to follow him around and stay near him, often sitting when he sits, rising when he gets up, and tagging along after him as the group moves from one feeding spot to another.

Gorilla fathers are curious about their new offspring, and they peek over the mother's shoulder to stare at their tiny infants. The new mother may let the male look at his baby, but she usually will not let him touch the helpless infant until it is much older. She mainly stays close to her male so he can protect her and their child.

CHAPTER 2

Dr. Nadler had plenty of questions about what had happened to Kishina, but nobody really knew the answers. He began writing to zoos and other research facilities all over the world. He was looking for information about why Paki may have rejected Kishina and about what had happened to other infant animals that had been abused by their mothers.

Kishina's body was thriving in the nursery at Yerkes, but it was her young mind that worried Dr. Nadler. He knew she belonged with other gorillas, not with humans. How long could Kishina be treated like a human before she actually believed she *was* one? Would Kishina ever be able to care for children of her own, or would she continue the cycle of abuse that began when Paki rejected her? Dr. Nadler was determined to come up with ways to help Kishina grow up as normally as possible.

A Gorilla Backpack

Until the infant gorillas are about two and a half years old, getting around is very easy for them. Mothers carry them in a "backpack position" until they are too old (and probably too heavy) for this form of transportation.

Everyone who cared about gorillas wanted answers to the same questions, because there were orphan baby gorillas in many zoos around the world. Only one mother gorilla in captivity had taken proper care of her baby. Field studies in Africa had shown that neglect and abuse almost never happened in the

Kishina went to live in the Yerkes nursery.

wild, so zookeepers and scientists knew something was terribly wrong with the way they were treating gorillas. What was it? Did the gorillas hate their cages or resent being confined in a small space? Was there something missing in their diet of gorilla chow, rice, vegetables, and fruit? Or were the gorilla mothers simply so inexperienced that they had no idea what to do with a wailing infant?

Zookeepers and animal specialists were puzzled over these questions. Most of all, they were worried about the health and safety of every gorilla infant that was born in captivity. So they took the safe way out. As soon as they realized a gorilla was pregnant, they put her alone in a cage, so she would not be "bothered" by other animals. After the birth, they tranquilized the mother and grabbed her baby so it could be raised in a nursery. Veterinarians, in particular, wanted to keep the infants in incubators so they would be warm. Without realizing it, these well-meaning people had been doing exactly the wrong things. Kishina's experiences ultimately helped point the way to better treatment of gorillas in captivity.

Of course, baby Kishina was too young to know what was wrong. Paki, her mother, may have felt bad because Kishina was gone, but she could not figure out what was wrong, either. If Paki missed Kishina, she certainly did not show it. She did not cry, or look around for the baby, or even seem sad; instead, Paki just kept pacing around her cage. Later, when she got back to her gorilla friends, Paki seemed to settle down. It was hard to tell if she even remembered her little girl. Perhaps she was just relieved to see her gorilla friends again and to be out of the lonely maternity cage.

Mike Ringer became Kishina's special friend in the Yerkes nursery.

I LIKE MIKE!

Since Paki seemed to forget about her new baby, Kishina really was an orphan. The caretakers in the nursery became substitute mothers and fathers for Kishina. Her favorite human was Mike Ringer, who became Kishina's special friend. Mike liked Kishina from the minute he saw her, curled up like a fuzzy, black ball in the nursery's plastic incubator. Like all the other orphan primate babies, Kishina had to stay in the incubator for at least three weeks. An incubator, which looks like a plastic

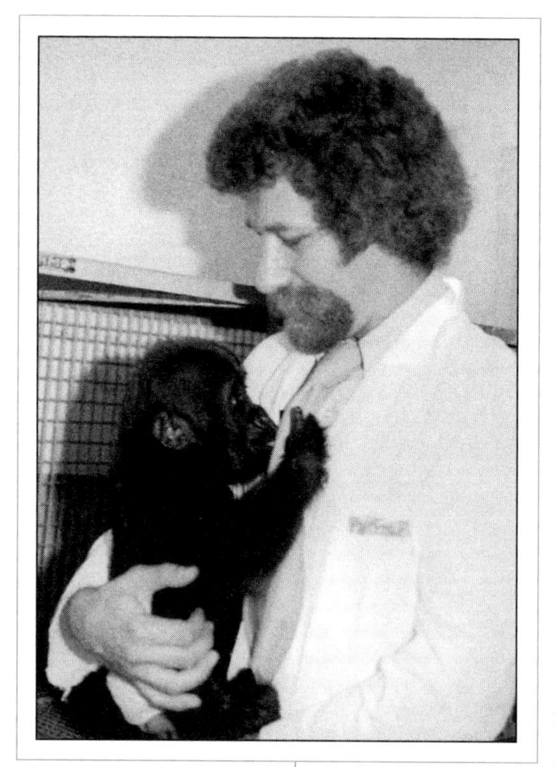

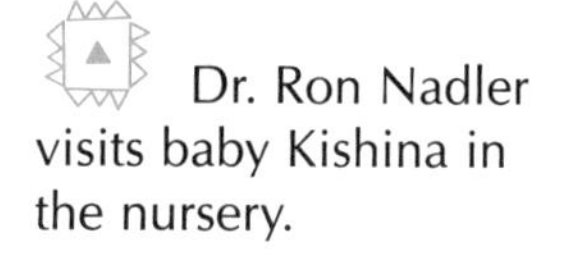
Dr. Ron Nadler visits baby Kishina in the nursery.

box, keeps babies warm. When the veterinarians said Kishina was big enough to come out of the incubator, they put her in a small cage. She could see and hear other babies, but could not play with them yet. But Mike was always there, smiling at her and holding her in his arms whenever he could. If Dr. Nadler wanted to know how Kishina was doing, Mike always knew the answer.

WHY WON'T KISHINA PLAY?

When Kishina could crawl, she moved into a bigger cage. This time she was not alone, because a playful baby orangutan became her cage-mate. Orangutans, or "orangs," have red hair and very long arms. Like gorillas, they are bright and like to learn about their surroundings. But Kishina did not play very much with the orangutan. In fact, Kishina seemed too sad to play with anyone at all. Gorillas are quiet animals, but Kishina seemed too listless and withdrawn.

Mike was the only person Kishina wanted to be with. Her day usually started at about 8:30 A.M., when Mike arrived in the nursery with an eight-ounce plastic bottle filled with SMA, a baby formula which also is used for human babies. Awake and wide-eyed, Kishina watched Mike silently, peering at him as she lay on her fluffy white and yellow towel. When he reached for her, she lifted herself up gladly and snuggled into his arms, gulping her formula and clutching at Mike's white jacket with her tiny hands.

After breakfast, Mike put Kishina into a "holding area" while he cleaned her regular cage. The little gorilla watched his every move. All the nursery attendants at Yerkes wore white jackets and pants and long brown rubber boots. Kishina felt safe around anyone who wore this uniform. If Mike could not pick her up, she would let the other attendants hold her on their laps while Mike was busy. But if someone came into the nursery who was not wearing the white uniform, Kishina whimpered with fear and scurried off. She hid in a corner, hunched over with her head down, until the stranger went away.

Kishina has an orang "roommate."

THE PRIMATE PLAYGROUND

Mike remembers Kishina's shyness, but he also says she was a sweet, cuddly baby. Her favorite pastime was being held in Mike's arms. From about 10 A.M. to 2 P.M., if the weather was nice Mike would take Kishina to the outdoor primate playground at Yerkes. The young animals romped on soft pine straw, climbed on jungle gyms, and rolled around in play-wrestling with one another. There were brightly colored balls, boxes, and tunnels for the little chimps, orangs, and gorillas to use, but all Kishina wanted to do was climb into Mike's lap and sit there, holding him tight.

While Kishina was outside, Mike often fed her a lunch of egg yolk, beef liver, carrots, cabbage, and green beans from little glass baby food jars. Her diet closely resembled that of a human baby. When she was old enough to chew solid foods, Mike gave her special treats of banana and apple. Kishina ate heartily, all the while staring at Mike's face and reaching for his white jacket so she could continue clinging to her favorite human.

GORILLAS AND HUMANS

Looking carefully at a gorilla–especially a gorilla baby–it is easy to see why some people think that chimps and gorillas are closest to humans in their physical makeup, hormones, and genetic traits. Many scientists believe that at the dawn of human history *Homo sapiens* (humans) and *Gorilla gorilla* (gorillas) had much in common but developed into two separate species. Both are primates, a scientific classification which includes humans, monkeys, and apes. Monkeys have tails. Apes (and humans!) do not.

NO CHIMPS FOR ME!

Sometimes, when all the baby apes were outside on a sunny afternoon, one of the young chimpanzees might waddle up to Kishina and try to get her to play. The chimp would poke at her and scoot away, hoping Kishina would follow in a game of tag. But Kishina did not want to play. Instead of romping with the chimp, or even swatting him away, she just got up and walked slowly to a corner of the playground, leaned her small fuzzy head against the fence, and stayed very still.

Baby Radi

Soon Kishina was not the only baby gorilla in the Yerkes nursery. Two more gorillas were born, taken away from their mothers, and raised by humans. One of them, Sim-Sim, was very inventive. He spent a lot of time throwing brightly colored balls against the fence around the outdoor playground or at the doors of the nursery when he was inside. Sim-Sim liked the thudding sound the balls made as they bounced off the doors.

Another young gorilla named Radi liked to play with the chimps. He was also very fond of people, especially Cathy Yarbrough, a public relations expert who worked at Yerkes and visited him often. Cathy tried to teach Radi how to pucker up his lips and blow a kiss. Radi tried, but he could not quite imitate his human friend; instead, he would scrunch up his face, blow air through his lips, and make a loud razzing sound. Every time he saw Cathy, he would give her the raspberry, making everybody laugh.

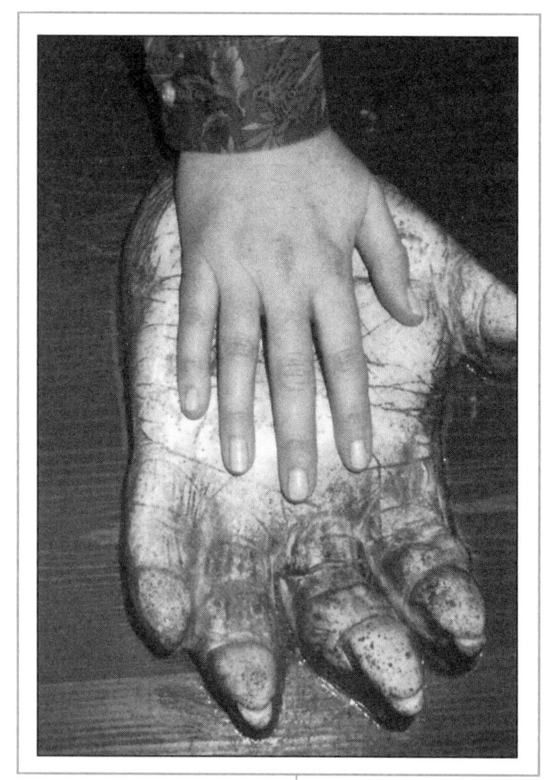

Gorilla hands are almost identical to yours, with a flexible thumb, a hairless palm, and translucent fingernails. But gorilla hands are much larger than human hands! This photograph shows an adult human hand against a plaster cast of a mature gorilla hand.

STARVED FOR AFFECTION

Kishina watched Radi and Sim-Sim, but she never joined in their games. As she grew older, she just hung on more tightly to Mike. Gorillas grow rapidly and gain great strength at an early age. When they are just toddlers—at about two years old—they are strong enough to cause trouble for a grown man if they want to, but Kishina was never disobedient or difficult to manage. She was just starved for affection, and now she had the muscle to hold so tightly to Mike that he sometimes could not pry her away.

When Mike wanted to leave the playground to go inside and do his work, he had to coax Kishina to let go of his white jacket. Then he would put her gently on the ground and make a dash for the door. Often, Kishina ran right after him, and if she was fast enough, she would grab his legs and hold tight. Mike was stopped in his tracks. He would pick her up, reassure the whimpering Kishina that he would be back soon, then try to put her down again and leave. Sometimes this had to be repeated four or five times before Mike could persuade Kishina to let go of him. And sometimes, she just would not let go at all. Then Mike would have to call another nursery worker to the playground to hold Kishina while he left. As he walked back to the building, he could sometimes hear Kishina crying for him, and her wails tore at his heart.

KISHINA MUST LEAVE THE NURSERY

Dr. Nadler's heart was aching for little Kishina as well. With every passing day, he became more convinced that she needed to be with other gorillas. She was being well cared for in the Yerkes nursery by people who loved her, and she was strong and healthy. But Kishina was becoming too dependent on human beings.

One day Dr. Nadler told Mike that it was time for Kishina to leave the nursery and move into an area with other gorillas, including Paki, Kishina's mother. Dr. Nadler and the other scientists hoped that the strong-willed mother gorilla and her shy little girl would be reunited.

That night Mike tossed and turned, thinking about Kishina. "I was glad for her," he said, "because it's good for a little gorilla to be with its own mother. But I was scared for Kishina, too. Suppose Paki got gruff with her? Suppose Paki even pushed her around, or hurt her? I was just crossing my fingers, hoping everything would turn out all right."

Muscle and Weight

Some gorillas may be as tall as humans, but they have a great deal of muscle, so they weigh much more. They are also much stronger! Male gorillas can reach a height of six feet, and weigh over 400 pounds. A gorilla this size could have the strength of ten men. Female gorillas are usually not more than five feet tall, and weigh about 250 pounds. They are also very strong.

Gorillas in the Wild

In the wild, gorillas spend their day in a slow, relaxed search for food, with plenty of time off for the adults to snooze while the youngsters wrestle and play at their feet. Sometimes the little gorillas play a game of chase, and they might even race across the sleeping body of a big male or jump up and down on his massive belly. The good-natured male will often let the babies use him as a trampoline. If he is annoyed, he will just gently push them off, turn over, and go back to his nap.

After traveling and looking for food all day, gorillas are ready to turn in early. As soon as the forest light grows dim, the family begins looking for a suitable place to spend the night. Family members sleep within hearing distance of one another, but the only gorillas who actually cuddle together all night are the mothers and their babies. Each gorilla makes a nest at night by bending plants into a circular pattern and lying down in the middle on the leaves. This forms a leafy "bowl" in the branches of trees or on the forest floor. A new nest, in a new location, is made each night.

Gorilla families travel within the specific area they claim as their territory, moving around so that food will not become scarce in any one spot. Once in a while two gorilla families bump into one another as they roam the forest. When that happens, the silverbacks of each family may get excited and roar, tear up small trees and wave them like clubs, or cup their hands and beat their chests rapidly. Chest beating does not make a thudding noise, but sounds like a huge woodpecker hammering at a tree–"pok, pok, pok, pok." Sometimes females will beat their chests, too, and the babies try to imitate them with tiny thumps.

This display of anger is usually a bluff because gorillas rarely fight. Instead, they hope the noise will frighten other animals and make them run away. It usually works. Gorillas also show they are upset by jerking their heads, charging, or simply by staring. That is why you should never stare for long at a gorilla; he or she might think you want to fight.

Gorilla family members may squabble over food or over who is the most important animal, but they almost always make up quickly. Then, they hug or touch one another as if to say, "I'm not mad at you any more." When they are happy and at peace with other family members, or when they see one individual they particularly like, gorillas will hum loudly, as if they are singing.

Ozzie and his son Kekla play together at Zoo Atlanta.

CHAPTER 3

Nobody likes to be moved to a strange place and separated from friends, but for the second time in her young life, this was happening to little Kishina. First, she was torn away from her mother, and now she had to leave Mike and the other young primates in the Yerkes nursery and go back to Paki. Would Kishina be scared? Would she scream and run away from a grown-up gorilla, even if it was her own mother?

Kishina was not ready for such a challenge, although she was now almost five years old. She was sturdy and plump, but she was still a very young gorilla. She was sharing a small cage with a lively baby chimpanzee named Jencie, but she stayed away from the other youngsters in the nursery, preferring only to play quietly with Jencie now and then. Kishina was still shy and afraid to assert herself. When Mike brought a new toy to the nursery, it was Jencie, not Kishina, who boldly grabbed it. When Kishina wanted attention from Mike, instead of wailing or demanding it like the others, she just hung on to him and whimpered.

When Gorillas Get Sick

When a gorilla gets sick its symptoms are just like those of a sick human. When Kishina was sick, she ran a fever and had a runny nose and cough. The Yerkes veterinarians treated her with ampicillin and other medicines a doctor might give a human toddler. More than other primates, gorillas really do act sick. When they feel bad, you can tell right away.

WILL KISHINA REALLY LEAVE THE NURSERY?

It is easy to tell when a gorilla is scared, excited, or even happy. A frightened gorilla may crouch, whine, or try to hide. When it is excited, it may run around madly and scream. A happy gorilla purrs, sits contentedly, and turns its mouth upward into a smile. Gorilla emotions seem to be very similar to those of human beings. That is why Dr. Nadler expected Kishina to be scared when she had to leave the nursery. He also hoped her mother, Paki, would be happy to see her little girl once again.

But Kishina and Paki had been separated for a long time, and Paki now had another baby daughter, Fanya. Dr. Nadler was glad that Kishina would be with a gorilla family. But at the same time he was concerned that problems might arise again.

Paki was caring for her new infant, but later would she grow restless and reject it just as she had rejected Kishina? After such a long separation, would Paki accept Kishina, her first daughter? Was Dr. Nadler doing the right thing?

The veterinarians were not sure. They had a lot of good reasons for wanting Kishina to stay in the nursery a little longer, protected by Mike and her other human friends. First, Kishina would be safer. In the nursery, no big animals could hurt a small gorilla like her. Second, the veterinarians said Kishina would be healthier in the nursery. She would be less likely to catch a

SURVIVAL IN THE WILD

Nobody knows how long gorillas live in the wild. Life is much more dangerous in the forest. Illegal hunters kill wild gorillas, while development destroys their habitat. Wild gorillas also die from diseases, injuries, or malnutrition. Gorilla babies are very weak when they are young, and if they do not get enough food or if their mothers cannot take good care of them, they will not live very long. Now and then two gorilla males bluff by acting very fierce, and as they rip up trees and rush around, they may accidentally hurt or kill a baby who cannot get out of their way fast enough. Almost half of the gorilla infants born in the wild do not survive.

cold or a more dangerous disease because the nursery was easier to keep clean. If she did get sick, the veterinarians could see her symptoms and treat her illness more quickly. Finally, they pointed out that baby gorillas grow faster—and bigger—when they are fed by humans and do not have to compete for food with other animals. Kishina would get more to eat in the nursery.

In the wild, mother and baby stay very close together for the first two years of the infant's life.

Maybe this was all true, said Dr. Nadler, but having Kishina grow up with a gorilla family was more important than anything else. If she was not reunited with other adult gorillas, Kishina might not be able to live with other gorillas in adulthood or to mate when she was ready. She could never contribute offspring to the world's rapidly vanishing supply of gorillas. There was much more at stake than just the life of Kishina. The survival of the entire species could be helped or hurt by what Dr. Nadler and the others at Yerkes did with this small gorilla.

His argument made sense. Dr. Nadler was now a world-recognized expert on gorillas, and his opinion was important. The veterinarians finally agreed with Dr. Nadler's judgment, and it was decided that Kishina would leave the nursery and go back to Paki.

The Growing-Up Years

For the first two years of life in the wild, gorilla babies stay very close to their moms. The mothers nurse their babies for those two years. Gradually the babies learn to eat different kinds of flowers, fruit, leaves, and other vegetation. Riding on their mothers' backs, the curious babies reach for the same foods the mothers are eating. Later they learn to find these foods on their own. Little by little, as a baby grows, it leaves the mother for short periods to climb a small tree or tumble in the grass with other young gorillas. It may also waddle up to other adult gorillas and try to play with them.

Dr. Nadler had another idea about the secret to a successful gorilla family. Maybe being a good gorilla mother was not so much a matter of experience or of watching other females take care of their babies. Maybe the mother needed to feel safe and protected by a male gorilla.

This thought excited Dr. Nadler, so he began to do more research. He knew that in the wild, gorilla fathers are always around to protect new mothers and their offspring. The mothers bring their babies to the male, sit next to him all the time, and follow him closely when he leads the gorilla group on food-gathering trips.

Dr. Nadler wondered if gorilla mothers in captivity could be good parents if they were allowed to stay with their mates. Gorilla mothers like Paki, who were forced to be alone or without their mates when their babies were young, often rejected those babies. Dr. Nadler hypothesized that the fear and insecurity caused by their isolation could be one reason some gorilla mothers rejected their babies. When the mothers had no mates and the babies had no fathers close by, raising a healthy child was difficult. Dr. Nadler's ideas were supported by an incident at the Cincinnati Zoo. When a mother gorilla began abusing her baby there, officials put her mate back in the cage. Reassured by the presence of the male, the mother gorilla picked up the baby and took care of it again.

THE STORY OF PATTYCAKE

There was also evidence that gorillas remembered their children after long separations. The evidence came from a gorilla family at the Central Park Zoo, in New York City. The mother was Lulu. The father was Kongo. They lived happily with their baby, Pattycake, in a sunny cage. Both Lulu and Kongo were gentle and affectionate parents. Together, they took excellent care of their daughter.

One day, however, a terrible accident happened. Kongo was in one cage, and Lulu and Pattycake were playing in the cage next door. Pattycake reached over to her father, and he took her hand. But Lulu did not see this, and she reached for Pattycake's other hand. For just a moment, the two parents pulled in opposite directions. Without knowing it, they broke Pattycake's arm.

A mother gorilla and her baby were reunited after a separation at the Central Park Zoo. Why couldn't it happen at Yerkes?

Pattycake had to be taken to the hospital, where doctors set her arm and put it in a cast. For the next three months, she lived in a nursery, just as Kishina did at Yerkes. There, fed and cuddled by humans, she grew very accustomed to all the special attention they lavished on her.

When it was time for Pattycake to be reunited with her parents, zoo officials and scientists in New York worried that she might react badly. They also feared that Lulu and Kongo might not remember their daughter or might not want her back. Dr. Nadler was asked to come to New York and help them reunite the gorilla family without any trouble.

Everything went perfectly. Lulu yelped with joy when she saw her daughter again, but she was gentle and did not try to push herself on the baby. Pattycake did cry a little when she saw her mother. She must have been overwhelmed by the unfamiliar sight of a huge gorilla, instead of the humans she had become accustomed to seeing, but the crying soon ended. When mother and daughter were comfortable with one another again, Dr. Nadler told the zookeepers to let Kongo come into their cage. The big male gently poked the baby, then bent to smell her forehead. Lulu sat very close to her mate, appearing to draw strength from his presence. Then Kongo marched around the cage, glaring at the humans who had gathered outside to watch. He seemed to be saying, "This is my family. Stand back, everybody, because I'm going to protect them!"

The Apes

There are four kinds of apes:

gorillas
chimpanzees
orangutans
(the great apes)

and

gibbons
(the lesser apes)

Apes all have hairy bodies and, unlike monkeys, they have no tails. Their arms are longer than their legs, and they have long fingers and toes. They also have relatively large brains and barrel-shaped chests.

REUNITED AT LAST

Kishina's father, Ozzie, was not around when the time came to reunite little Kishina with Paki. But Dr. Nadler believed that Kishina needed to belong to a gorilla group, even one without a father. "Kishina couldn't stay in the nursery another day," he recalls. "She needed to start learning about gorillas and how to get along with them as an adult. If she didn't, she would not even know she *was* a gorilla."

So, Kishina moved from the nursery into her mother's cage. At first, when Kishina timidly looked up and saw Paki, she whimpered and hugged herself in fear. Paki sat quietly in a corner, but she still looked huge and muscular. Kishina crouched close to the floor

Even though Paki was not very welcoming, Kishina and Fanya enjoyed playing and cuddling together.

and trembled. Paki did not seem very interested in her older daughter. She hung back, poking instead at her new baby, Fanya. Little Fanya toddled over to Kishina and gazed at her with curiosity. She seemed to take pity on Kishina and patted her on the head.

Paki also walked slowly over to Kishina, but she just glanced at her and sniffed. Kishina crouched even lower. Paki did not seem to like what she saw—or smelled—because she grunted with displeasure and ambled away.

It was baby Fanya who finally broke the ice. She grabbed her older sister playfully and gave her a hug.

Kishina and Fanya watch Inaki eat, maybe hoping for a bite of banana.

Kishina responded with a squeal of delight. Fanya was tiny, just like some of the other young apes Kishina had known in the nursery. Kishina felt better. She was not afraid of little Fanya! For the rest of the day, the two sisters romped together, while Paki watched quietly. She had accepted Kishina, and was not going to hurt her, but she did not seem thrilled to have her back. Maybe mother and daughter had been separated too long.

From then on Kishina was part of a gorilla group, but she never did get much attention from her own mother. Paki either ignored Kishina or was mean to her. Paki grabbed all the food, stuffing it into her own mouth while Kishina watched hungrily. Kishina began to grow thin because Paki would not share food with her. When Kishina tried to play with her mother, Paki chased her away. Only baby Fanya seemed to like Kishina.

After a while, it became obvious to Dr. Nadler that too much time had passed, and Paki was not interested in nurturing her first child. He moved Paki to another group and put two other female gorillas in with Kishina. One was shy Inaki, a small, chubby gorilla who would become Kishina's lifelong friend. The other was a sweet-tempered gorilla named Oko. Both of these gorillas seemed to enjoy having Kishina around; they played with her, sat close to her, and never snatched her food away. Finally, Kishina had a home with adult gorillas who could give her what she desperately needed: companionship.

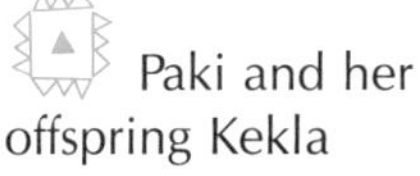
Paki and her offspring Kekla

GORILLAS NEED COMPANIONSHIP

In the time that had passed since Kishina's birth, scientists had learned a great deal just by watching her. They discovered many things that link humans to gorillas, such as the need for a family, the devotion that mates have for one another, and the importance of a father in making the mother feel secure. Perhaps most striking, however, was the discovery that in order to be normal and healthy, gorillas, like humans, need companionship.

Dr. Nadler was convinced that baby gorillas, like human infants, need the constant touching, holding, and protection of their mothers. In turn, the mothers did best in giving this attention when their mates were close by.

Choomba stays close to the newborn Kudzoo in the Ford African Rain Forest.

LOVE AND ATTACHMENT

Gorilla fathers watch over their toddlers and take care of them when the mothers want some time off to rest or eat. If the mother dies or leaves her family for some reason, the father may take over the parenting chores to make sure his baby survives.

In human terms, the word "love" means many things and is shown by physical contact, loyalty, trust, and respect. In the animal world, love can be described as "attachment." Certain animals become very attached to each other and feel sad and lonely when they are separated. Babies who are denied contact with the objects of their attachment become shy and scared. Had this happened to Kishina?

"Gorillas who don't get this experience don't seem to know how to act around others of their own kind," explains Dr. Nadler. "I think the need for companionship is built into the psychology of the gorilla. As long as a gorilla has the security and attention it needs, it can respond to nature and become a good parent. We wanted Kishina to have this chance, and that's why we hoped she could get the experience she needed from other gorillas."

Scientific Method

Scientists look for facts to help us understand the world we live in. In this case, Dr. Nadler was trying to discover the best way to care for animals in captivity. When scientists begin to investigate a problem, they usually follow a procedure called the Scientific Method.

These are the steps in the Scientific Method:

▲ State the problem

▲ Gather information

▲ Suggest a hypothesis (a possible answer to the problem)

▲ Perform an experiment to test the hypothesis

▲ Record and analyze data (the facts) from the experiment

▲ Reach conclusions based on the information from the experiment

When these steps are completed, the scientist forms a theory (an explanation of or solution to the problem) or decides to search for more information.

Gorilla Development

Like humans, gorillas grow in stages. Every human child seems to go through the same predictable growth patterns: infancy; early childhood; early adolescence; the teenage years; and finally, adulthood. With gorillas, the progression is much the same. They are born after a gestation period of eight and a half or nine months—about the same amount of time a human baby spends in the uterus.

Gorilla babies are helpless at birth and spend the first few months of infancy nursing, sleeping, and cuddling close to their

mothers for warmth and protection. Later, if it is healthy and normal, the gorilla will gradually mature at a very predictable rate. For example, it will crawl at the age of about two months, walk on all fours when it is four months old, and be considered a "toddler" ready to leave its mother's side for play by the age of one year. Gorillas are considered to be infants until they are three years old. From ages three to six they are called juveniles, or "children." Males are sub-adults between the ages of six and eleven; females are sub-adults from ages six to eight.

By age eight or nine, a female gorilla is ready to be an adult. An eight-year-old human, by contrast, is still very much a child. So, maybe one way to compare yourself to an ape is to think of a gorilla your age as being much more socially mature. The gorilla is ready to accept the responsibilities of being an adult—in its own world—much faster than a human.

A gorilla's sexual maturity comes much faster than a human's, as well. When the females reach the age of eight, they are adults and can mate and have babies. Males can mate at about age eleven, but that is still a bit young for gorilla fatherhood. The males usually do not fully mature until they are around fifteen. At that time, you can tell they are about to become "dominant," or mature males, because the hair on their backs turns silver and they become known as "silverbacks."

Females do not get silver hair on their backs, but the hair on their faces turns gray as they get old. (It does in males, too).

In addition to the silver hair on their backs, mature gorillas develop a ridge over their eyes and a crest running along the top of their heads. The crest is made of bone and is called a sagittal crest. They need this skull structure to support their big, heavy jaws. Females also have brow ridges and crests, only smaller.

As a male gorilla ages, the hair on his back turns silver.

CHAPTER 4

Kishina felt at home with her new gorilla group. She lost some of her shyness and developed a hearty appetite, which helped her grow. Kishina was smart; she knew what was going on around her, and she flourished in this less confining atmosphere. Dr. Nadler's dream for Kishina had come true: at last she was not afraid of other gorillas.

GROWING UP GORILLA

The scientists thought the time for her to have a mate and a family of her own was drawing near. Like other gorillas, Kishina did not pay much attention to the opposite sex until she was about six years old. At that age, she was beginning to feel and act like a human teenager. Kishina began teasing some of the young male gorillas, and they enjoyed teasing her back. Kishina loved to play hide-and-seek with the males; she would dash to a corner of her cage and scrunch up against the wall, hoping that the male could not see her. Of course, he always did, and he would announce his discovery with a loud yelp of delight. Kishina answered with "Heh, heh, heh." It sounded very much like a giggle.

Calabar, Kishina's mate and the father of her first child, Kinyani

KISHINA HAS A BABY

When it came time for Kishina to mate, not just any male gorilla would do. She needed a very special companion. When she was nine years old, the age of young womanhood for a gorilla, Kishina was introduced to a male named Calabar. He had a broad chest and enormous shoulders, with the characteristic male sagittal crest over the top of his head.

Calabar was much bigger than Kishina. He weighed over 400 pounds, while Kishina weighed only about 180 pounds. His swaggering and bold nature contrasted with Kishina's shy, soft personality. But the two got along very well, because as big as he was, Calabar was gentle with Kishina. Joel Volpi, one of the researchers at Yerkes, said, "It's lovely to see Calabar with Kishina.

He likes her, really likes her. He treats her so well. No lunging, no bullying."

Kishina responded to Calabar's good manners with what could only be described as gorilla "love." They didn't live in the same cage, but side-by-side in adjoining cages, so Kishina could visit Calabar whenever she wanted. Dr. Nadler would often watch the two young gorillas with a big smile on his bearded face, thinking, "Little Kishina has certainly grown up into a fine young lady."

Soon, Kishina and Calabar began to mate regularly. In July, 1982, Kishina became pregnant. On a chilly spring morning in 1983, Kishina gave birth to a baby girl named Kinyani, from the Swahili word for "ape-ish." To avoid the mistakes of the past, Dr. Nadler insisted that Kishina not be alone. Despite the research Dr. Nadler had done, some veterinarians refused to believe that putting Calabar with Kishina would be safe. As a compromise, Kishina's best friend, the sweet Inaki, was allowed to stay with Kishina for help and support. Kishina would not have to be puzzled or lonely during her first, difficult days of motherhood.

Kishina turned out to be a much better mother than her own mom, Paki. She cuddled Kinyani and made sure that the stick-thin infant was wrapped warmly

The adult male sagittal crest is easy to see in this photograph.

in her arms every minute. She let Inaki look at the baby, but she allowed no touching. Kishina was a jealous and protective mother around other gorillas, but she enjoyed letting people "ooh" and "ahh" over Kinyani. When a human came to visit, Kishina rushed to the front of her living quarters with Kinyani in her arms. Then she sat down, as close as possible to the visitor, and opened her arms to reveal the tiny infant.

Inevitably, the human would praise Kishina for having such a fine baby. Kishina drank it all in, relishing the attention and excitement of the moment. If the visitor had gum, candy, fruit, or any other treat to offer, Kishina accepted it as if she were certainly entitled to a reward!

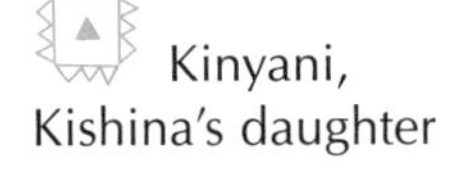
Kinyani, Kishina's daughter

At last, Kishina truly had a family of her own. She seemed settled and happy. But changes loomed on the horizon that would directly affect Kishina. Across town, at the zoo in Atlanta, workers were busily digging the foundation for a new animal exhibit. It was being built especially for gorillas.

THE NEW ZOO

The new gorilla home at the Atlanta zoo was being built primarily because of one energetic man with a love for all animals and a special place in his heart for gorillas. He was Dr. Terry Maple, a Georgia Tech professor of psychology and an expert in animal welfare. Dr. Maple agreed to become Atlanta's zoo director in 1984; things started looking up for all the animals almost immediately. Workers tore down cages and built huge outdoor compounds where the animals could roam. People enjoyed visiting the zoo much more when they saw how happy the animals were.

Dr. Maple knew that gorillas did not belong in cages, either at Yerkes or at any zoo. Dr. Maple had studied gorillas, both in captivity and in the wild, and had great respect for their intelligence, their gentle personalities, and their close kinship to humans. He believed the only way to preserve these marvelous primates in an artificial or manmade habitat was to make sure they were free to live in family groups with other animals they really liked, so that they would breed and produce plenty of babies.

Dr. Maple and the Yerkes director at that time, Dr. Frederick King, decided to get together and create a new home for the Yerkes gorillas and for the only gorilla at the zoo, a huge old male named Willie B. The zoo, now renamed Zoo Atlanta, would build a new home for all the gorillas. It would be a fine, large outdoor compound where they could live almost as if they were in the forests of Africa. When it was built,

ATLANTA'S RAIN FOREST

The Ford Motor Company donated over one million dollars to make the dream of a new gorilla home at Zoo Atlanta come true. In honor of the donor, it was named The Ford African Rain Forest.

Dr. King would allow many of the Yerkes gorillas to live there. One of those animals would become the mate of Willie B.

There was only one catch—Kishina could not go to the zoo.

The scientists already had decided to send Paki, Kishina's mother, and other animals related to Kishina to the zoo. The scientists did not want too many gorillas with the same "gene pool"—gorillas from the same immediate family—to breed at the zoo, because it might produce unhealthy babies. Kishina's sister, Fanya, had already left and was living at the Audubon Zoological Parks and Gardens in New Orleans. Paki and Calabar would go to Zoo Atlanta, but Kishina had to stay behind. Kishina was unaware that soon she would be separated once again from the gorilla friends she knew and loved.

Willie B. at Zoo Atlanta

THE STORY OF WILLIE B.

Before the arrival of the Yerkes gorillas at the new habitat, Willie B. was the only gorilla living at the Atlanta zoo. Willie B. was captured in the forest as a toddler, and he spent the next twenty-seven years of his life alone in a cage at the zoo. He had not seen another gorilla since he was captured, and his only friend was his human keeper.

Willie B. had a big tire swing in his cage, and even his own television set. But companionship is important to a gorilla, and no amount of toys or television sets can make up for the lack of a family. Willie B. was lonely and bored.

Choomba cuddles the newborn Kudzoo.

When the new gorilla living area was completed, Willie B. was let out of his cage for the first time in twenty-seven years. When he came blinking into the sunlight, he also saw his new family: fifteen gorillas from Yerkes. Among them was Kishina's daughter, Kinyani, who was now almost seven years old. Kinyani and some other members of Kishina's beloved gorilla group were romping in the grass, playing tag among the trees, and relishing every second of their newly found freedom.

Willie was about twenty years older than Kinyani, but he responded to her the minute he saw her, and the two soon began to mate. Everybody was thrilled and hoped they would have a baby. But Kinyani was apparently too young to bear children, so Willie B. turned his attention to a twenty-seven-year-old female named Choomba. For a long time, they just sat and stared at one another. Finally, they mated, and Choomba became the mother of Willie B.'s first child.

HOW TO NAME A BABY GORILLA

When Willie B. and Choomba's baby was born, Zoo Atlanta decided to let the people from Atlanta name the little gorilla. They had a big "Name the Baby" contest. The winning name was "Kudzoo." This name is a play on words that any Southerner will recognize: kudzu is a fast-growing vine that covers much of the South.

When he saw how happy all the gorillas were, Dr. Maple said he felt like crying with joy. Dr. Nadler was also very happy for the animals—except for Kishina. She was still in a cage, back at Yerkes. Would Kishina ever be free?

Sim-Sim was one of the young males at Yerkes with Kishina.

KISHINA WANTS TO BE THE BOSS

There simply was not enough money or space at Yerkes to build a big outdoor area for the gorillas like Kishina, who had been left behind when the others moved to Zoo Atlanta. But with Dr. Nadler's help, the scientists figured out a way that the animals could at least be together; they let Kishina and five other gorillas have the run of three adjoining cages. The side doors to these cages were left open so the animals could go inside to stay warm or outside to get some sun. They also could visit

Willie B. lounges in the Ford African Rain Forest.

freely with one another. It was not ideal, but it was the first time Kishina was with a group consisting of both males and females. The other gorillas in Kishina's group were: Rok, a big male who was sick a lot and who suffered from mental retardation; Kishina's old friend Inaki; two young males, Sim-Sim and Makini; and Pojo, a big, tough female who was another of Kishina's sisters.

In every gorilla family, there are both dominant and submissive animals. The oldest and biggest male is the dominant male. His favorite mate is usually the oldest and most experienced female, and she is the dominant female. The younger animals are submissive, which means they allow the dominant animals to have their way and to lead the family.

Kishina was getting older now, and she had lost much of her youthful shyness. One day she decided that since she was a mature female with plenty of strength and experience, she should be the dominant animal. There was no dominant male in Kishina's new family, so she tried to be boss by being the dominant female.

But Pojo also wanted to be boss. Pojo snatched Kishina's food, glared at her, and challenged Kishina's bid to be the dominant animal. Ultimately, Kishina was no match for the strong-willed Pojo. So Kishina spent a lot of time playing with Sim-Sim, who was young enough to act like a curious child and who did not make Kishina feel insecure. Kishina also felt pretty good around Makini, who was a little older than Sim-Sim but still immature and willing to let Kishina boss him around. Rok was too ill to present a challenge, and Kishina tolerated him with kindness. But around

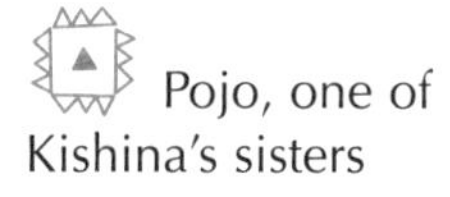
Pojo, one of Kishina's sisters

Pojo, Kishina was still timid and fearful. She would rather spend time with humans, accepting their gifts of fruit, than strut up to Pojo and compete with her for the title of "boss." When Pojo came near, Kishina reverted to her old, shy self, losing her confidence and slumping in the corner, defeated.

A PLACE FOR KISHINA

Meanwhile, Dr. Nadler was studying the gorillas at Zoo Atlanta, and he was delighted by what he saw. Paki had another baby, a little male named Kekla. Many other gorilla babies were being born, too. Dr. Maple, the zoo director, was right; putting the gorillas in a natural habitat could encourage reproduction and help to save the species. Partly because the gorillas were doing so well, and partly because Dr. Maple was recognized not only as an animal expert but also as a top-notch administrator, people soon began to call Zoo Atlanta one of the best zoos in the country.

Still, while the other gorillas enjoyed their wonderful home at Zoo Atlanta, Kishina remained in her cage. It seemed as if she would get few rewards for being such a good research animal. She had been responsible for the happiness of so many other gorillas, but she still had a long way to go herself. Dr. Nadler and Yerkes director Dr. King realized this, and they worried about it. Was there another place Kishina could go where she, too, could feel free?

Can Gorillas Learn To Speak?

Gorillas sit up, crawl, and move around on their own earlier in life than human babies. This physical superiority is surpassed, however, by the greater ability of a human to learn language. Apes can develop a capacity for language skills, although their capacities are much less than those of humans. A grasp of language makes it possible for humans to pass on history to their children and to realize and tell others that things are going to happen in the future.

Many animal researchers think gorillas have the mental capacity to "talk." They certainly communicate with one another through a series of whines, cries, chuckles, purrs, roars, and body language. These verbal gorilla-to-gorilla communications are called vocalizations. There are at least fifteen vocalizations that scientists have recorded as recognized "gorilla language."

In captivity, a gorilla who wants to show affection for a particular human may hum, or "sing," when that human comes near. Some caretakers say this sounds like a giant kitten purring!

Signs And Symbols

Two researchers at Georgia State University, Duane Rumbaugh and Sue Savage-Rumbaugh, have demonstrated that higher primates—chimpanzees, for example—do grasp symbolism and can get their feelings and needs across through the use of a symbolic language called "Yerkish." The chimp studies were started at Yerkes, and the knowledge gained from the experiment has helped some mentally challenged human children learn how to express themselves.

Both chimps and gorillas apparently have the intelligence to talk, but what stops them from making sounds we can understand is that these animals do not have the voice-box, tongue, or jaw structure needed to create human speech. Even so, certain gorillas have been taught to communicate in other ways.

A female gorilla named Koko, who lives with her mate at a research facility in Woodside, California, was said to have learned to "speak" on a near-human level through the use of sign language. It is the same sign language used by people who are deaf. With her massive hands, Koko "signs" words and sentences that suggest she has thoughts and feelings very similar to a human's.

The Story of All Ball

Koko became famous when one of her human friends gave her a kitten. Because the kitten had no tail, it looked like a furry round ball to Koko. Koko named the kitten All Ball. She cuddled All Ball and treated it like her own baby. When All Ball died, Koko wept and signed to her human friends that she was very sad. The story was in many newspapers, and people were amazed that this gorilla not only displayed such deep feelings, but could also communicate those feelings to others. Koko eventually got another cat, and was kind to this animal, too. She is reportedly able to have conversations like this:

Human, pointing to the letter C in a book: *"What letter could that be?"*
Koko signs: *"C"*
Human: *"Yes, you're right. Is there a word you know?"*
Koko signs: *"That cat." (points to the word CAT in the book)*
Human: *"Yes, correct."*
Koko signs: *"Tiger that. Tiger cat."*

CHAPTER 5

There *was* a place for Kishina. This time, it was not exactly a zoo, but an animal park with a fine reputation for conservation, for the breeding of endangered species, and for teaching people about animals. This animal park is Busch Gardens in Tampa Bay, Florida. The officials at this spectacular park wanted a gorilla exhibit, but they did not want to take the animals from the forest. Every time a wild gorilla is taken out of its forest home, a gorilla family is separated. The captured animal also suffers sadness, mourning over the loss of its companions and its home. For these reasons, the officials at Busch Gardens decided to look for gorillas for the new exhibits among gorillas already in captivity.

The people responsible for bringing new animals to Busch Gardens took a look at the way Yerkes and Zoo Atlanta had cooperated on the Ford gorilla home, and they liked the idea. Busch Gardens could build a special, forest-like outdoor compound for gorillas on land it already owned. People would come from all over the world to see this recreated forest, and to watch the gorillas romp, play, and eat very

Preserving the Food Supply

A mountain gorilla group's home range may extend thirteen to nineteen square miles. The gorillas do not strip the vegetation from one spot. Rather, they eat only a moderate amount, leaving behind plenty of shoots that can grow up by the time they pass through the area again.

much as they do in the wild. This new exhibit would also encourage gorillas to mate and reproduce, thus helping to save the species.

Dr. King and the other scientists at Yerkes were willing to make a bargain with Busch Gardens, similar to the one they had with Zoo Atlanta. Build a fine new home, they said, and we will allow you to have our gorillas live there.

Among others, Kishina would travel to the new habitat in Florida. At last, she could live outside of a cage!

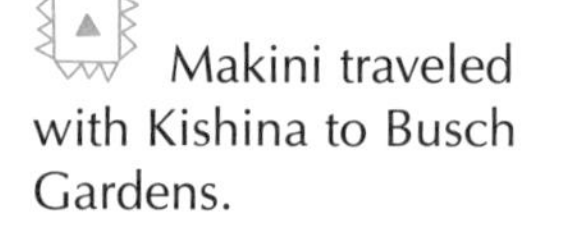

Makini traveled with Kishina to Busch Gardens.

A NEW HOME

The trip to Busch Gardens was hard for Kishina. At dawn on April 15, 1992, she and the other remaining gorillas at Yerkes were bundled into wooden crates, which were then rolled into two trucks. The animals, wide-eyed and restless, moved uncertainly around in the hay scattered on the floor of the crates. Several of Kishina's favorite humans were with her, including primate care technician Sammie Hughley, veterinarian Karen Ihde, and Yerkes public information officer Cathy Yarbrough. They offered her oranges and spoke to her in calm, soothing voices.

But how could Kishina know what was going on? How could the humans tell her there was no danger, and that she was going to a wonderful new home? They could not make Kishina understand, so Kishina trembled with anxiety. Gorillas do not enjoy new situations and this was a very big change for them.

"DON'T BE SCARED, KISHINA"

"Don't be scared, Kishina," Sammie said over and over. The trucks sped to Tampa Bay as fast as they could. Bumping along inside were Kishina, Inaki, Pojo, and the two little males, Makini and Sim-Sim. Rok, who had a weak heart, had died of a heart attack a few weeks before the move.

All the gorillas began to sweat from fear and from the rising heat of the day. Gorillas do sweat, particularly when they are scared. The males, especially, give off a strong odor when they are uneasy. Kishina was sweating too, and she seemed nervous and afraid.

Finally, the trucks rolled into Busch Gardens, and the gorillas were transferred to a large, air-conditioned indoor suite that had been constructed just for them. The animals had "bedrooms" and a huge play area. Big windows opened to enticing views of their future outdoor compound, and Kishina could see young men and women spreading oranges, bananas, peanuts, and other treats on the grass just outside the windows. She started to relax.

Climbing Trees

Gorillas in the wild can usually find enough food on ground level, but if necessary, they also can climb into trees to collect fruits or flowers. They have very large molar teeth to grind up their food.

When the doors to the outside compound finally opened, Kishina was the first to rush out and explore this new home. She scrambled over to a tree, and touched it tenderly. It was the first time in her life that she had ever been this close to a tree! She could feel the wind in her hair, and the sun warmed her back. She bent down, running her hand over the sweet-smelling grass. Then she walked slowly to a bright red hibiscus flower, looked at it with a puzzled grin, and pulled. When the flower came off in her hand, Kishina cocked her head, unable to understand how she had done this. Realizing that the flower belonged in the ground, she tried to "replant" it by pushing the bloom back into the earth. Watching, Cathy Yarbrough laughed and gave Kishina the nickname of "the Gardener." Kishina seemed to love all the brightly colored foliage in her new home.

Lash, the dominant male at the Myombe Reserve

GORILLA PARADISE

Kishina's home at Busch Gardens was called the *Myombe Reserve: The Great Ape Domain.* In addition to the five gorillas from Yerkes, a mature male named Lash came to live at Myombe. Everyone thought Lash would be the dominant male in this new family and that the dominant female, and Lash's mate, would be Kishina.

Myombe encompasses over an acre of lush forest, plus indoor rooms where the animals go to rest at night. Myombe smells, sounds, and looks just like a real tropical forest. There is even a mist that rises in the morning, just as it does in a real forest. Gerald S. Lentz, vice president of zoological operations at Busch

Gardens, says he wants this area not only to enchant visitors but also to serve as a place where gorillas will breed. Kishina's new home is so amazing that many visitors say Myombe seems like a gorilla paradise.

Kishina's favorite spot at Myombe is a small clearing among thick gray rocks, just above a waterfall. She perches there contentedly, watching the dancing veil of white, bubbling water, her thick body framed by the purple flowers of a Hong Kong orchid tree. Shiela Wood, the young woman who is the chief gorilla technician at Myombe, says Kishina claimed that spot because it is the best place to catch the fruit treats Shiela throws to the animals each afternoon. It is also a great way for Kishina to relax while peering down at her human visitors.

Kishina "the Gardener" enjoys her new home.

KISHINA LOOKS RIGHT INTO YOUR EYES

In the short time that she has been at Myombe, Kishina has developed great confidence in herself. Her old timid personality is gone. At last, Kishina is bold and self-assured. She has even been able to show Pojo that she really is the boss, and the two females finally act as if they respect one another. The fact that Kishina sits in the best spot, and that none of the other animals dare to snatch her food (although now

Kishina in her favorite spot at Myombe Reserve

and then she takes theirs), shows that Kishina has finally emerged as the dominant female. Everyone at Busch Gardens hopes that she and Lash will mate and have children.

"Of all the gorillas, Kishina is the one who can look you straight in the eye," says Shiela. "This tells us she feels secure. Kishina sits there and actually seems to study humans. She takes her time and concentrates. She has become bold."

A TYPICAL DAY

The day at Myombe begins at seven o'clock in the morning, when Shiela comes into the bedroom quarters to say hello. She looks over each gorilla for watery eyes, a runny nose, or any other sign of illness. If a gorilla looks sick or does not want breakfast, Shiela plays it safe and calls a veterinarian. Most of the time the animals are playful, wide awake, and hungry. This shows that they are healthy.

At 8:00 A.M., Kishina gets two or three cups of warm, nonfat milk and oatmeal. Then comes monkey chow, biscuits made of corn meal and other grains. They look like giant shredded wheat, without the sugary frosting. When the monkey chow is gone, Kishina gets about a pound of vegetables and fruits, such as celery, broccoli, pears, apples, and peanuts. She picks out the peanuts and apples first, because these are her favorite breakfast foods. She eats slowly, and with great relaxation. The meal usually takes about twenty minutes.

Pojo and Kishina, now friends, live together at Myombe Reserve.

At nine in the morning, visitors to Busch Gardens begin arriving, and all the gorillas go outside. Kishina often struts right up to the visitors' window, smacks it hard, and then dashes away. It is her way of asking the humans to play with her, and they almost always do. If Kishina sees someone whose face interests her, she will press her body against the glass and stare at that person. Unlike other gorillas, her gaze is long-lasting and unafraid; she doesn't consider a stare hostile or threatening because she is comfortable around people. (After all, humans were her "parents" in the Yerkes nursery!)

When Kishina tires of playing games with her human visitors, she wanders off into the trees and shrubs of the compound or spreads out for a nap right in front of the windows. While some big male gorillas snort and grunt loudly in their sleep, Kishina sleeps soundly and quietly.

Between 11:00 A.M. and noon, one of the eight gorilla experts who care for Kishina and the others at Myombe scatters oranges and other treats in the grass. They want the gorillas to forage for the food, as animals do in the wild. This keeps the gorillas alert and curious.

In the afternoons, especially when it is very hot, oranges, grapes, sunflower seeds, and other healthy snacks are mixed together and frozen in big cubes. Then this frozen treat is also scattered around. Kishina has figured out that these "gorilla popsicles" usually land near her favorite spot above the waterfall. She goes there in the afternoon so she can be first to catch the treats without having to dash around for them.

Gorilla Diet

In the wild, a gorilla's diet consists mainly of the following foods:

- ▲ shoots, leaves, and stems of plants
- ▲ a small amount of fruit (about two percent of their diet)
- ▲ occasionally a few slugs or grubs

Sometimes, gorillas also will eat soil that is rich in calcium and potassium if their bodies need extra boosts of these nutrients.

Gorillas of Myombe: Sim-Sim (top), Kishina (left), and Inaki (right)

A BIG, RELAXING DINNER

Each evening, the gorillas return to their indoor bedroom area to relax and enjoy a big dinner of sweet potatoes, vegetables, biscuits, milk, and more fruit. They are usually fed by Tonya and Ed or other gorilla experts they know and trust. Kishina and the other gorillas want the same human friends near them all the time. Strangers who come very close can make them nervous, so visitors usually are not allowed into the bedroom area.

"This is their turf," says Ed. "Everything we do around their inside or outside home is for the gorillas. If they want to play we'll play, or if they want attention—a back scratch or some soft talk—we will do that. Our job is to make the gorillas happy."

Just before Kishina and the others go to sleep, they have "enrichment time." Toys are brought out

Napping in the Wild

About a quarter of a gorilla's daily schedule consists of resting. During heavy rain showers, gorillas huddle together under the leafy roof of the tropical rain forest.

that are specially made for gorillas: balls, bamboo shoots, or a long block of wood with holes that are stuffed with peanut butter. Kishina loves this food-toy; she pokes her fingers into the holes to scoop out the peanut butter. The toys are another way to keep the gorillas busy and alert. They are so smart that they would get bored if they did not have lots of new and exciting things to look at, play with, and figure out.

After playing for a while, the gorillas drift off to sleep. Each gorilla makes a nest out of the straw and other soft, clean materials put out for them at night. They can sleep alone or with another animal, as they wish. Kishina often nestles next to Pojo. Now that it is clear Kishina is the dominant female, there is no more competition between the two and they have become good friends.

What Do Gorillas Drink?

Because they get the moisture they need from food, gorillas rarely drink. One of their favorite snacks is celery sticks, which contain a great deal of water. Sometimes, however, gorillas soak the back of their wrists with water and then lick it off.

KISHINA LOVES ATTENTION

All of the gorillas, both at Zoo Atlanta and at Busch Gardens, are unafraid of humans and seem to welcome their smiles, the pointing of cameras in their direction, and the cries of delight from visitors when the animals approach. But of all the gorillas, Kishina loves attention the most.

Kishina is especially interested when people take notes in front of the big windows. She is fascinated by writing, as if she cannot quite figure out the magic of a little stick (a pen or pencil) making marks on paper. As at Zoo

Atlanta, researchers come to Busch Gardens to observe the gorillas, and they often write in their notebooks, while Kishina stares at the pages. Once, one of the gorilla experts gave Kishina an old telephone directory to play with. When she saw someone writing, Kishina grabbed the telephone book, opened it up, and pretended to write, too.

Kishina also likes to play with her human visitors. She often prances up to the big windows which separate humans from the gorillas in one spot of Myombe. Sometimes, she picks out one child from the group and plays chase, or she might bang on the window and wait for the child to bang back. Kishina also enjoys lying on her back in front of the windows, putting straw on her face, and waiting for people to laugh.

▲ Author Maxine Rock and Kishina communicate through the glass at Myombe Reserve.

Kishina also knows how humans communicate nonverbally, and she has managed to pick up some human body language. She winks, nods, gestures, waves, and scrunches her face into a smile or a frown. Tonya, one of her human friends at Busch Gardens, says Kishina believes that humans are kind and expects them to treat her very well.

"She always wants attention," Tonya says. "If she doesn't get it, she looks at you with real disgust. It's as if Kishina is saying, 'What's the matter with you? Don't you know I'm special?'"

KISHINA'S LEGACY

Kishina is broad-shouldered now, and she weighs about 250 pounds. A patch of reddish-brown hair on the very top of her head makes Kishina look as if she is wearing a jaunty cap. She always has a soft, placid expression on her broad face, as if she cannot stop smiling.

A great deal of what humans know about gorillas is due to Kishina. Dr. Nadler studied her at Yerkes and published the results of his discoveries so other scientists could share the knowledge. As a result, people learned how to care for gorillas in captivity. From the moment Kishina came into the world, she gave people the answers they needed to help her species. Kishina taught us about what gorillas need.

Scientists and veterinarians have come to realize that gorillas, like humans, need a family and should not live alone. They finally understand that baby gorillas must stay with their mothers and learn from interacting with other gorillas. Because of Kishina, we can all appreciate much more about gorillas, especially their intelligence, devotion to family, and their gentle personalities.

Kishina

The Endangered Rain Forest

The rain forest, where most wild gorillas live, got its name because it is often damp and misty. Almost every afternoon during the two rainy seasons, a brief storm drenches the forest. The gorillas huddle together in the rain, looking chilly and miserable, but they usually do not seek shelter from the storm. Maybe that is because it is over so fast. When the sun glitters brightly again, there are huge raindrops clinging to the green leaves of the forest trees. When the gorillas pass beneath the leaves, they shake off the drops, which spatter down as if it was still raining.

Gorillas eat over 200 types of plants that grow in the trees and on the ground in the rain forest. The gorillas move slowly on the ground in the soft forest light, as rainbow-colored birds tweet and whistle above. The wild pigs, elephants, leopards, monkeys, and other animals that share the forest with the gorillas do not fear them. Although they will occasionally eat an insect, gorillas are primarily vegetarians, which means they will not kill and eat other creatures. Instead, they spend most of their time looking for leaves, fruits, nuts, berries, and roots. Gorillas usually leave the other animals alone.

Not many animals bother the gorillas, either. Very rarely, a leopard or other predator (an animal which hunts others) may grab an unprotected baby gorilla and eat it. Mostly, however, the gorilla's worst enemy is man.

Many humans want to make money from destroying the rain forest. Farmers say the land should be cleared and converted to farms. Ranchers want their livestock to graze on the rich forest vegetation. Loggers cut down the trees and sell them for lumber. Miners, hoping to find precious metals, dig up the soil and create huge wounds in the earth.

All of this human commercial activity takes a terrible toll; about 140 square miles of tropical rain forests are ruined each day. If this continues, the forests of some countries will be gone in about thirty years, and the remaining wild animal habitats may be too small to support many gorilla families.

Gorillas, especially, suffer from rain forest destruction. Big animals need a lot of food, but they cannot get it if humans keep destroying the forest. Also, as more and more people invade their forest homes, the gorillas are shot by illegal hunters. Some of the hunters want to make trinkets out of gorilla body parts to sell, and some think that medicine made from gorillas can cure illness. (It cannot.) Some hunters even eat gorilla meat! In the past few years, several gorillas died from wounds they suffered as a result of stepping on land mines soldiers placed along forest paths. Some rain forest areas are battlegrounds for feuding tribes, and the gorillas are becoming the innocent victims of war.

Like humans, gorillas reproduce very slowly. Not enough wild gorilla babies are born each year to make up for the gorillas that die in the forest.

We can't afford to lose a single gorilla, because there are so few of these gentle giants, either in the wild or in captivity. Only about 35,000 lowland gorillas and 450 mountain gorillas still roam the sweet-smelling rainforests. That's not very many! There are about 500 gorillas in zoos and animal preserves. The U.S. Fish and Wildlife Service lists gorillas as an endangered species. That means if humans don't help them, all the gorillas may soon disappear.

CHAPTER 6

Of course, animals like Kishina should be left in their natural homes. But now that gorillas are an endangered species, zoos, animal parks, and nature preserves can help gorillas in their fight to survive.

A good zoo or preserve comes as close as possible to letting gorillas live as if they were free, while at the same time keeping them safe. In the wild, diseases kill many gorillas before they can produce offspring; in a good zoo or preserve, experts can watch over the animals and care for them when they get sick.

Gorillas in the wild also have been threatened by poachers, greedy people who ignored the law and hunted down wild animals to sell their skins or other body parts. This sort of poaching has been greatly curtailed, but there are other dangers for the gorillas. Local hunters, who have always supported themselves by hunting and who may have difficulty finding another way of life, also invade gorilla habitat. Gorillas sometimes get trapped in snares meant for other animals. Some African governments try to stop the poachers and hunters, but it is a frustrating and costly job.

The biggest problem faced by the gorilla population, however, is loss of habitat. As the human population increases, people use more and more

Why Zoos Are Important

A good zoo or animal park is much more than a place you can go to see animals. It also:

▲ Makes sure the animals are content, well fed, medically cared for, and housed in areas that come as close as possible to the way they would live in the wild.

▲ Serves as a breeding place for animals, in the hope that endangered species will not become extinct.

▲ Provides a place where scientists can study animals and learn more about them.

▲ Helps children and adults learn about animals and develop a greater appreciation for nature.

▲ Teaches people to be kind to animals and to take care of Mother Earth.

▲ Encourages foreign nations to cooperate in zoo projects.

▲ Inspires artists to paint pictures of nature, encourages writers to do stories about animals, and helps people create all kinds of art centering on animals.

▲ Helps schools and universities teach about conservation and wildlife.

▲ Lets people relax and have a good time.

space, and they gradually take over the wild places like the rain forests. They cut down the trees so they can graze cattle, grow crops, and build new homes. This leaves little remaining wild areas for the gorillas.

AN EXPENSIVE AND DIFFICULT TASK

Taking care of captive gorillas is exciting and important, but it is also expensive and difficult. Most zoos and laboratories abide by international agreements not to remove gorillas from the wild, so if they want to buy a gorilla from another zoo or lab, they must pay about $200,000 just for one animal.

Paki, Kishina's mother, at Zoo Atlanta

To take care of that animal, they need gorilla experts, "keepers," veterinarians, and others who know about the animals and are willing to give them hours and hours of loving care. Feeding the big gorillas costs hundreds of dollars each week. Their medical bills, for everything from colds to surgery, are close to what it costs for doctors to take care of a human. Just building a suitable home for a family of gorillas costs more money than most human families will ever have; for example, the Ford African Rain Forest at Zoo Atlanta cost $4.5 million.

There are only about 260 gorillas in Canadian and American zoos, but officials at these zoos are trying very hard to make sure the gorillas have a chance to raise their own families. To do this properly, all responsible zoos and wildlife parks got together to form what is known as a Species Survival Plan. Under this plan, the zoos cooperate to match gorillas to suitable mates and to regulate the breeding and treatment of the animals.

Just as humans can be identified by their fingerprints, gorillas can be identified by the unique pattern of their nose wrinkles.

To make sure the animals are treated well, zoos follow certain rules and allow inspectors on the premises to see if they are keeping their promises. Every good zoo gets a "seal of approval," which is called accreditation. The group that accredits zoos in the United States is called the American Association of Zoological Parks and Aquariums. Both Zoo Atlanta and Busch Gardens, where Kishina now lives, are accredited by this group and participate in its Species Survival Plan.

Kishina is in a wonderful home in a natural habitat facility like Busch Gardens, but not all gorillas are so lucky. Some gorillas will be hurt or killed by cruel or ignorant humans. Some people advocate returning all animals now in zoos and animal parks to the wild. But they may not realize what problems await the animals, such as hunters, war, or habitat destruction. Humans take up more room and destroy more of the earth's wild places every day. Can we reverse the damage to the animals' natural habitats?

It seems that as long as there are humans on earth, some of them will make mistakes with nature and animals. But as long as animals are on this earth, some other humans will try to correct those mistakes.

Perhaps you will be one of those other humans.

WHAT YOU CAN DO TO HELP

You can show kindness and concern for gorillas by realizing that every individual—including you—can make a difference. Many people sympathize with the plight of the gorilla but think they cannot really do anything to help. But you can! Here's how:

▲ **Learn all you can about gorillas.** Action begins with information. Go to the library and get books and articles about gorillas and their habitat. Learn about the dangers that threaten them in the wild, and why zoos and animal parks may be one of their chances to survive. The more you know, the more other people will listen to you when you talk about gorillas.

▲ **Talk to other people about gorillas.** When you think you have enough information, help others learn about gorillas, too. Each person who understands the dangers to gorillas and gains new respect for these animals can join in the effort to protect them.

▲ **Visit the zoo often.** Become a "regular" at your local zoo and make a point of visiting good animal parks whenever you can. When you are there, notice the way the gorillas (and other animals) are housed: are they in cages, or do they have sunny outdoor compounds? Are they alone or with others of their own kind? If you do not like what you see, ask a guide or the zoo director what is going on and why.

▲ **Study conservation displays.** A good zoo will educate people, not just entertain them. Look for displays that tell you about the animals, where they came from, what they eat, and if they are endangered. When you see a zookeeper, ask questions about the animals. Make every zoo trip an educational—as well as a fun—experience.

▲ **Join the zoo "family."** Most zoos have a membership group that gives you discounts on admission, entitles you to receive a zoo magazine or newsletter, tells you the inside scoop on what is going on at the zoo, and may even give you a chance to take special trips with animal experts. Ask about such groups and join one if you can.

▲ **Adopt an animal.** At many fine zoos you can join an Adopt-an-Animal program. For a set amount of money, sometimes paid once a month, an individual or a group can help with the bills for a gorilla's food and medical needs. Some zoos offer special photos of your animal and a chance to take behind-the-scenes tours at the zoo.

▲ **Write letters about gorillas.** Write to your local newspaper to point out good or bad things about the zoo and to help others learn and care about gorillas. Write to legislators who make laws helping the rain forests.

▲ **Don't buy products made from endangered species and don't buy any animal taken illegally from the wild.** There are laws against selling certain wild animals, such as gorillas, but some people do not obey them. Remind your parents and other adults that a good pet shop will follow the laws and not sell animals or animal products which are illegal or endangered.

▲ **Learn about and support groups that are trying to protect endangered wildlife.** Wildlife conservation groups press for habitat conservation and for laws protecting endangered animals.

Although gorillas are found primarily in the rain forests of Africa and in some other limited tropical regions, they have human friends all over the world who are trying to help them survive.

Dian Fossey Fund One group working for gorillas is the Dian Fossey Gorilla Fund. Their newsletter, "Digit News," is named after a friendly male gorilla named Digit who was killed and cut apart by poachers so they could sell his hands and feet for ashtrays. Digit was one of the gorillas studied by Dian Fossey, the scientist featured in the book and movie *Gorillas in the Mist.*

World Wildlife Fund This is another group dedicated to helping gorillas (and other wild animals).

African Wildlife Foundation The African Wildlife Foundation also raises money to protect gorillas.

There are many other groups like these in the United States and in other nations. Watch for their literature in the mail. Some of them are devoted to all wildlife, some are only for gorillas, and some are interested mainly in other rare and endangered animals.

People *will* listen to a well-informed young person who is sincerely trying to help the animals. The keys to being effective are:

- to have the facts,
- to present them calmly and with conviction,
- to be patient and kind when you explain things about gorillas. In this way, you have a good chance of convincing people to help in the fight for gorilla survival.

Epilogue

Dr. Terry Maple
Director,
Zoo Atlanta,
Atlanta, Georgia

Children are not afraid to communicate with gorillas on a basic level: with smiles, cries of excitement, and joyful laughter. Children and gorillas understand one another because they are both free of guile and openly trustful. They are also both eager for affection and quick to embrace a friend.

Kishina, the gorilla in this book, has been a true friend of humans. Born and raised in a laboratory and forced by circumstance to live apart from her own kind in childhood, Kishina learned to love the people who took care of her. Later, when she was reunited with some members of her gorilla family, she was able to bridge the gap between the world of humans and the world of gorillas.

Kishina let us study and learn from her from the time she was a mewing infant. She never became impatient, gruff, or bored. Gently, with the wisdom and grace that seems to be built into the personality of all gorillas, Kishina led her human friends on a voyage of discovery. Through her, scientists all over the world learned how captive gorillas mate, reproduce, and care for their young. Without Kishina, we may not have succeeded in helping these magnificent great apes survive in a world that has become increasingly dangerous for wild animals.

At the turn of the century, gorillas were virtually unknown. They lived hidden deep in the jungles, peaceful and safe. Humans invaded their territory and nearly wiped them out. Today, places like Zoo Atlanta and Busch Gardens (where Kishina now lives) are trying hard to save the species in the wild. The lessons we learned from Kishina are helping us toward that goal. Scientists at the Yerkes Regional Primate Research Center, and Dr. Ronald Nadler in particular, initiated the behavioral studies and also made valuable contributions toward improving the lives of gorillas in animal parks. Many of the gorillas we have at Zoo Atlanta came directly from Yerkes.

We have eighteen lowland gorillas at Zoo Atlanta. Seven of them are Kishina's relatives. Her mother, Paki, lives here, and so does her father, Ozzie. Kuchi and Kekla are siblings of Kishina. She also has three half-sisters here. They are Mia Moja, Stadi, and Kashata, all of whom were fathered by Ozzie.

I have been privileged to know gorillas and the people who study them. It is our strongest hope that together we can create a world that is safe for gorillas and the many other creatures who occupy the rain forest. Gorillas are surely among the world's most charismatic wildlife. We must do all that we can to save them.

Kishina, I salute you. You have my thanks, and my admiration. I promise to keep trying to help your relatives here at Zoo Atlanta, and wherever else humans are lucky enough to come in contact with gorillas.

A Note From Busch Gardens

Gorillas are delightful, majestic animals. It has been my privilege to know a number of gorillas during my zoo career. We now have six of these magnificent animals, including Kishina, at Busch Gardens Tampa Bay, and I continue to enjoy them and to marvel at them.

Kishina and four of her gorilla companions from Yerkes have met and now live with Busch Gardens' male gorilla, Lash, in a lush tropical setting. It was very rewarding to see the Yerkes animals explore and accept Myombe's outdoor world of grass, bushes, flowers, and trees. All of the gorillas have completely accepted Myombe as home.

Busch Gardens is grateful to Yerkes for their trust in us. Working together, we hope to successfully expand our knowledge of gorillas and the gorilla family at Busch Gardens. We thank Maxine Rock for telling Kishina's story and emphasizing the threats facing gorilla survival in the wild. Unfortunately, it is quite clear that gorillas and many other endangered species require the efforts of zoos and other controlled environments if these species are to survive and avoid extinction.

GERALD S. LENTZ
Vice President Zoological Operations, Busch Gardens Tampa Bay, Florida

Timeline of human knowledge of gorillas

470 BC	Ancient Phoenician writings describe apelike forest creatures called "gorillai" seen on an expedition to western Africa.
1700s	Sailors and explorers bring tales to Europe of hairy beasts seen in the forest.
1770s	Linnaeus arranges the animal kingdom in categories and places apes in the order PRIMATES.
1847	Dr. Thomas Savage writes a description of gorillas gathered from the inhabitants of West Africa.
1850s - 1860s	French-American adventurer and explorer Paul Du Chaillu writes exaggerated stories of his encounters with gorillas in the Congo forest.
1860s	British explorer John Hanning Speke searches for the source of the Nile River and reports tales of gorillas living in volcanic mountain forests.
1896	Richard L. Garner from Harvard University attempts to study gorillas in the wild from the safety of his iron cage.
1902	Captain Oscar von Beringe of the German colonial government brings back the body of a gorilla shot in the Virunga region; scientists name it *Gorilla gorilla beringei*, the mountain gorilla.
1902 - 1925	Many gorillas are shot by hunters and collectors.
1911	First gorilla is exhibited in a United States zoo.

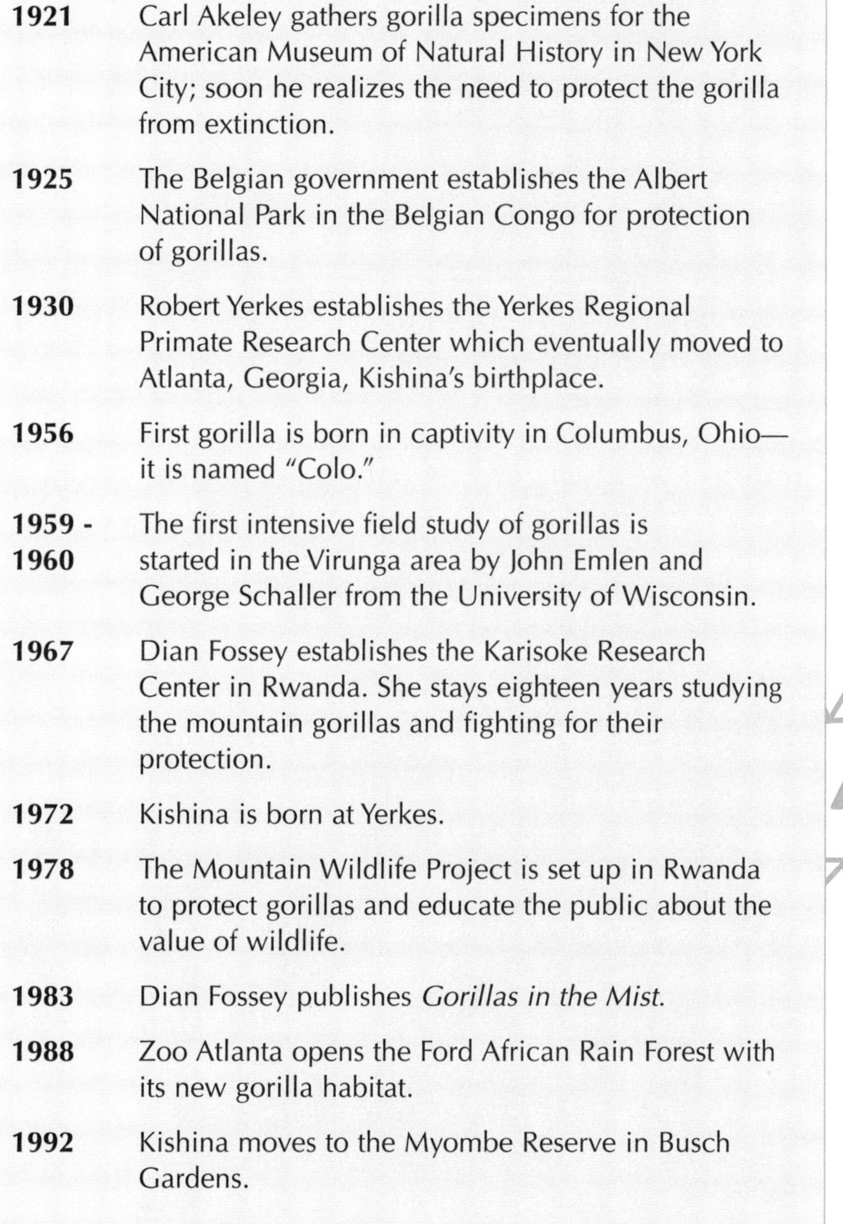

1921 Carl Akeley gathers gorilla specimens for the American Museum of Natural History in New York City; soon he realizes the need to protect the gorilla from extinction.

1925 The Belgian government establishes the Albert National Park in the Belgian Congo for protection of gorillas.

1930 Robert Yerkes establishes the Yerkes Regional Primate Research Center which eventually moved to Atlanta, Georgia, Kishina's birthplace.

1956 First gorilla is born in captivity in Columbus, Ohio—it is named "Colo."

1959 - 1960 The first intensive field study of gorillas is started in the Virunga area by John Emlen and George Schaller from the University of Wisconsin.

1967 Dian Fossey establishes the Karisoke Research Center in Rwanda. She stays eighteen years studying the mountain gorillas and fighting for their protection.

1972 Kishina is born at Yerkes.

1978 The Mountain Wildlife Project is set up in Rwanda to protect gorillas and educate the public about the value of wildlife.

1983 Dian Fossey publishes *Gorillas in the Mist.*

1988 Zoo Atlanta opens the Ford African Rain Forest with its new gorilla habitat.

1992 Kishina moves to the Myombe Reserve in Busch Gardens.

GLOSSARY

Calabar

Calabar — Kishina's mate at Yerkes and father of Kinyani, her daughter

compounds — man-made areas in which an animal lives

conservation — a careful protection of something, especially an animal, to prevent its destruction or harm

dominant — in charge, in control; in a gorilla group, the older and bigger animals are usually dominant

endangered — threatened with extinction

GORILLAS ARE FOUND IN THE WILD ONLY IN AFRICA.

There are three kinds of gorillas:

Gorilla gorilla gorilla *western lowland gorilla* Fewer than 35,000 are thought to survive. They have short hair, usually blackish gray, but sometimes brown. They inhabit the forests between western Cameroon and the Zaire River. The lowland gorilla is the type usually seen in zoos and animal parks.

Gorilla gorilla graueri *eastern lowland gorilla* They have short black fur and longer faces. Most of them live in the lowland forests of eastern Zaire.

Gorilla gorilla beringei *mountain gorilla* This is the rarest type of gorilla. According to a recent census, the number of these gorillas is around 450. These animals, recognizable by their long, silky, black hair, live on the slopes of the Virunga Volcanoes, in Rwanda, Zaire, and Uganda.

gene pool — a collection of genes in an interbreeding group that determines the characteristics of the individuals in that group

gestation period — the time that a baby stays in its mother's uterus

habitat — the place or area where a plant or animal naturally lives

Homo sapiens — the scientific species name for human beings

hypothesize — to make a tentative assertion or guess in order to test its truth

Kinyani — Kishina's baby by Calabar; this name means "ape-ish" in Swahili

Kishina — Swahili word meaning "the source"

Myombe Reserve — the natural habitat at Busch Gardens in Tampa, Florida, where Kishina now lives

natural preserve — an area restricted for the protection and preservation of natural resources, such as animals, trees, or plants

Paki — Kishina's mother

poachers — illegal hunters who kill wild animals to sell their skins and other body parts

Pojo — Kishina's sister

Kinyani

Kishina

Paki

Pojo

predator — an animal that hunts and eats other animals

Ozzie

Ozoum — Kishina's father; called "Ozzie"

rain forest — a tropical woodland with large evergreen trees that form a roof of leaves

silverback — mature male gorilla; this name comes from the silver hair on the gorilla's back

submissive — the gorillas in the group who follow instead of lead the other animals

theory — an idea or procedure based on scientific fact; a hypothesis which gains support from evidence

vocalization — verbal gorilla-to-gorilla communication, which includes purrs, growls, and other noises

Yerkes Regional Primate Research Center of Emory University — the scientific research center in Atlanta, Georgia, where Kishina was born and raised

Yerkish — a symbolic language learned by some apes

Acknowledgments

Books are complicated. No author can do it alone. This book had special help from many wonderful people, and I would like to thank them on this page. They are:

The late **Dr. Geoffrey Bourne**, who first introduced me to the Yerkes Regional Primate Research Center of Emory University, and to the gorillas; **Dr. Frederick King**, former director of Yerkes, who served as mentor and friend; and **Dr. Thomas Insel**, the current Yerkes director.

Dr. Ronald D. Nadler, Research Professor of Reproductive Biology, who was determined to help Kishina and her species, and without whom this book would not be possible.

Cathy Yarbrough, Chief of Public Affairs for Yerkes, who helped every step of the way with the miracle of Kishina.

The other delightful people at Yerkes, especially Chief Superintendent **Jimmy Roberts** and his staff.

Dr. Terry Maple, who works a few miracles of his own, including bringing Zoo Atlanta to the top as one of the nation's ten best zoos.

The incredible people at Busch Gardens, whose love for animals shines in everything they do, especially **Gerald Lentz**, Vice President for Zoological Operations, **Shiela Wood**, Curator of Great Apes, and the staff who cares for Kishina.

Photo Credits

The Author and Publisher wish to thank the following for the use of their photographs throughout this book:

Courtesy of Wildlife Conservation Society: page 6
Courtesy of Busch Gardens Tampa Bay: pages viii, 36, 39, 44, 46, 54, 55, 56, 83, 85, © 1995 Busch Gardens Tampa
Courtesy of Frank Kiernan: pages 1, 17, 22, 38, 52, 82, 84
Courtesy of Ronald D. Nadler: pages 3, 12, 14, 15, 29, 30, 83
Courtesy of Cathy Yarbrough: pages 25, 57, 59, 61, 63, 71, 83
Courtesy of Maxine Rock: 13, 18
Courtesy of Zoo Atlanta/Sebo: pages 9, 31, 32, 34, 40, 42, 43, 45, 48, 65, 69, 73, 74, 83

Index